U1

MW00931160

Confronting 22 Years of Pain Held Captive

by

Paris Cashmere Pruitt

The I.M.P.R.I.N.T Initiative
Connecticut

ISBN: 978-1-72104-416-0

Front Cover Design – Deka Henry
Interior Illustrations – Deka Henry
Editing – Chrismine Brun, Tiana Robinson, Jasmine N. Skinner
Formatting – BoardHouse Publishing
Print

Printed and bound in the United States of America.
First printing August 2018

www.theimprintinitiative.com

This one is for you, whoever you are in this moment. Whoever you need to be in this moment. This book was written to grant you peace of mind in your hardest moments. Don't break, don't fall, always stand tall. Pain is temporary and change is constant so if you continue to grow, you will grow through your pain.

Table Contents

I hope you find peace in words. I hope that my words are seeds for growth.

— Jm

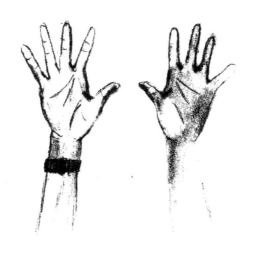

The Journey

Hartford born and raised until she was snatched before my eyes.
Next stop Florida, where I learned life can be full of lies.
Dragged through the dirt 4 times, but the 5th time I rise.
On a journey to break the chains from the minds that history has vandalized.
Created to value the plan the oppressor devised that crucifies and implies that we are unwise, but the truth is here.

I AM ALIVE.

Living without You

The darkness that comes over you when death comes is something
you cannot prepare for.
I thought I would be able to see her when she went home
Because that is what always happened.
She was strong so she would make it through
But I got the call and I didn't make it in time
She was gone and I didn't get to say goodbye.
Second time it was her other half.
I wrote all the wrongs through him.
We just couldn't fill that very void.
I cried for months and pushed everyone away.
All I wanted you to do was see me cross that stage.
I still struggle everyday, but I know you both are watching over me
so I will be straight.

Rape Culture

Stay away from him.
Don't let him near when the days become dim.
These are the words spoken about monsters in your family.
Everyone knows that they can do something to children but not their baby.
It's impossible to say they won't or are incapable of doing it to one child and not another.
There is immense trauma that is held within when someone takes your innocence.
It's not a coincidence that a child becomes quiet or even violent.
They can't tell anyone what happened.
Because all your life you heard the words "I will kill anyone that hurts you".
That won't make a child develop to be open and honest
And if this is you don't be afraid to be you.
Don't let this situation make or even break you.
Seek help to live your life.
Don't let this chew your view of what you were sent to this Earth to do.

The Comfort of Chaos

A whirlwind was created because I trapped my pain inside.
I tried to blind my mind with all the trauma I held inside.
But I just destroyed people and places around me because I didn't see the signs.
I couldn't see that chaos was destroying me, I just kept it close to me.
It took me so many times of self-destruction until I finally realized, I was inviting lies.
No one wants to live a chaotic life but it became my comfort place so much that I didn't want to be in another space.
Now I don't miss the chaos I dismissed, I am now falling in love with peace of mind.

I am a Black Lesbian Woman

I always felt your presence but you were never welcomed by anyone around.

I always wondered why everyone wanted to keep you down.

I introduced you to mom dukes when I was one- five but she dismissed you as a chapter that didn't need to be alive.

She didn't understand that killing you would have been the abortion that she had planned.

She tried to ignore your very existence because she couldn't stand what had began.

She tried to disconnect our bond by shrinking my air way one second at a time.

I think she thought the tighter she held around my neck that you would be released at anytime

This moment should have been enough for me to never search for you again

But shockingly in that moment I knew you were a real one, most genuine sin

The more I explored you I started to love you unconditionally

Because you are me and I am you

Matter of fact I think this is my cue

Hello world this is,

scratch that

I am the Lesbian identity that everyone shows a blind eye to

I will never neglect you because I cannot be a powerful Black Woman without you

I will be proud to be you in the room of homophobic white supremacist

I will be proud to be you in the room of homophobic black religionists

You chased me for so long it's time for me to chase you

You stood true to me when I neglected to even know you

For this I will educate those that are unwise to the true depths that lies within the core of this Black Lesbian Woman before your eyes

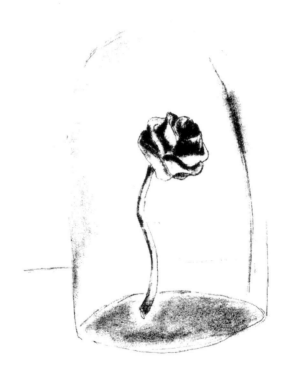

The Power of the Black Woman

She loves but never finds love
She reflects beauty, flipped outside or in
She is dipped in gold, with a glow so rare
She is the one that birthed this nation
She is a descendant of exploitation
Her image is only seen as annihilation
She comes in many ways shapes and forms
She is Angelou in the mind
She is Baartman in the body
She is Shakur in the soul
She is the Truth in Tubman who took steps years before the march on Washington
A bystander they depicted her in HIStory textbooks written by white AmeriKKKa
The only time she stood by was when her body was seen as a mere spectacle
She was seen as a freak show later on as a freak hoe
But words couldn't stop her, she belongs to the largest group of college graduates to occur
And still they think she is illiterate because her use of Ebonics
Anything she has created will never be hers, because Becky will be there to steal it
They stare at Kylie Jenner's lips or Kim's thick thighs
But forget to cite the true author of these twos' lies
I bet if Michelle switched the roles and was the performer of Melania's words ...
Do I even need to say more
When they said me too, they forgot to say Burke
Damn she is really hurt
Sometimes she wants to snatch her cape off because of the racism, ridicule, and the rape
She needs an outlet for her pain
So she wrote this for you, yes you sis in the back, with the rich melanin skin and locs flowing down your back
Keep shining and keep smiling and I really need to see you win
Because I am my sisters' keeper tomorrow today and always have been

Identity Crisis

I am sorry if I ever neglected any of you
I just couldn't be black as a lesbian woman
I just couldn't be a lesbian as a black woman
I just couldn't just be a woman as a black lesbian
However, one of you always wasn't welcomed
When they said Black Lives Matter they didn't mean you all of you.
Truly they didn't mean any of you.
But you still push the black agenda
You still raise your fist in the air for injustice
You still promote inner city transformation
When will they give you a hand, the world may never know.
Will you keep fighting alone?
Will you keep crying alone?

Love in Plain Sight

I heard the whisper of the air when we first met.
It pushed us both back.
Back and forth because it was not suppose to happen like that.
But now when I look into your eyes,
I see a Queen's light brighter than your highlight.
Broken from life, you picked up my pieces ready to put them all back.
I pushed and you pulled because I was not sure what you had done to me.
Through our hardest of times I rested my head on your neck with your nails sunken into my back, and your legs gripped me ready to attack.
But all in the same moment something felt wet, a tear rolled down your face.
A feeling came over two and made one.
Love was the one and two, the rawest feeling that we could have ever meet.

School Days

Remember when you used you to get A's
Yeah those were the good old days.
Now all you see are C's maybe even a D.
But I can't stress the transcript.
I am going to build relationships.
Because I was once told, the only thing that feeds the soul is the who not the what.
Find your passion and purpose so you can be free.
Free from failing the standard that they think you need to be.

Knowledge is Power

When I found you I was desperate.
I needed a real escape route.
Would I be who I am without you?
It worked for me to dive into Junie B. Jones life and to leave Paris C.
Pruitt behind.
I will be chasing a piece of paper that won't mean anything if I am
not free.

Because when you look like me, you have to talk, walk, and speak
like them.
Because the higher you go the farther they think you will fall.
Because the first place that they take from is the education fund.
So you want me to come into the world unknown to me and get this
degree.
Because I can still come to college, get a degree, and be free.
Because when you earned that F, that was a recipe for your success.

I will rise, soar, and fly because I didn't need education in the first
place.
I used the knowledge I had when they stripped my education away.
I couldn't give up because I had something within
You gave me the willpower to fight, to win.
**So let me have that P with the h on the side and yeah you might
as well throw that D right behind**
And I am pulling up to college that my ancestors built with their
blood, sweat, and tears with the hope that one day I would shine.

Therapy

Sitting down in an empty room, staring, and talking about feelings.
How can I even get with this, you're a stranger?
And I have told you things that the closest people to me don't know.
I was told that I was too strong for you
Or I never needed it, prayer would help more
Or last but not least I only needed you to change my sexual identity.
But you have shown me that it's okay to open my soul
I can't run from my pain.

Locs

I sometimes feel as though you failed me.
I expected you to grow and look the way I wanted without
maintaining.
Imagine you went untouched for 10 weeks
How would you adjust?
Imagine if I weren't loved.
How would you look?
Imagine if there was no time allotted to care for you.
How would you feel?
Course, and utter disgust.
You would fall out and thin like the rest.
If you didn't nourish your physical being the way that you should.
How do you expect us to nourish from the root if you feed us with
poison?
Just think about that.

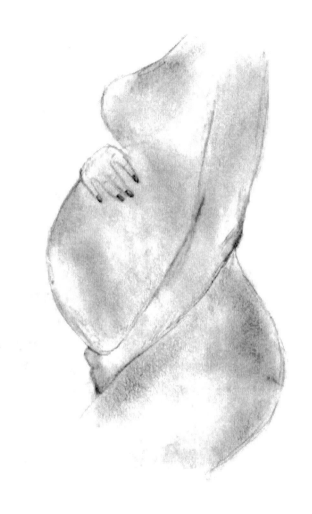

Mom Dukes

Carrying me in your womb for 9 months, so strong.
Pushing me out of your vaginal canal for the third time, so amazing.
I don't know a person in this world stronger than you are.
Never force yourself somewhere you don't fit, words written on my
heart.
I never realized but I saw you cry once, a gift and a curse.
The foundation of black womanhood is to carry the loads of
everyone around us.
The person that gave me life,
I plan to make your wildest dreams come true.

Sperm Donation

Sperm donation was your contribution to my life.
You taught me how to spit anger and neglect any one else's opinion.
I gave one too many chances.
But I will live a better life without you.
The chapters of my life that you were included in are painful.
But I would never say that I wish I never knew you.
You allowed me to know my most natural relationships in my life.
Thank you for your family, but see you when the universe believes
the alignment is necessary.

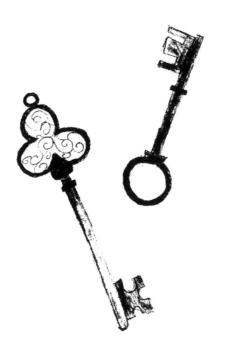

Advice to You

Confidence is key to fully embrace the pieces of yourself that you don't want the world to see.
Loyalty is the hardest thing to find but love won't work without it.
Believe in your greatness that you have within, success is in your reach.
Trust that you will find a love that won't break you.
You can't distance yourself from the people that want to see you win the most.
Speak up even if you are alone in the fight.
Mental stability is hard to find but you are strong enough for this fight.
Don't lose yourself so young you cannot find yourself when you grow old.
Be yourself, people will love you anyway.

Learning History to Write Our Story

Our ancestors dreamed of the day, this day in particular.
Not when life would be a breeze but when we would align with their dreams.
To stop putting our lives in the hands of another and help one another.
Tubman didn't just free the ones biologically connected to her.
She freed the racially identical.
There was a sense that I am you, you are I, and we are one.
We have to regain this spirit and build each other up to dismantle the curses bestowed on us by our colonizers.
It doesn't matter if you are light or dark, hair straight or kinky.
We have to see each other as equals because no matter the complexion, we are still in the same section.
We are helping in the fight to break our people.
So, let's teach our black children to love themselves in whatever way they come.
Build their minds to create a grind of buying back our communities one project at a time.

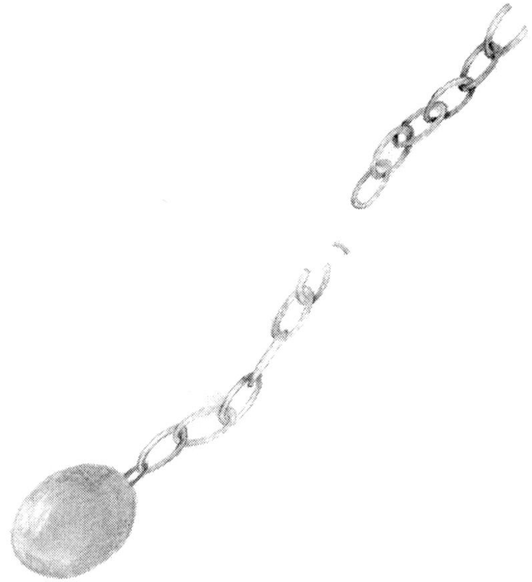

Buy Black Our Communities

Who owns our communities?
Not me, and definitely not someone that looks like you.
The projects are operated to keep us contained.
Then they make it a maze and make us run into a trap and call it a
house.
The importation of drugs caused for the deportation of great minds.
**This is when they reintroduced us to the chain gang, new prison
gang, I mean that new day slave game.**
No matter how you see it the justice system begins to own you.
They start taking your rights from you, animalizing you.
Once you become a slave to this system, you won't get hired, be able
to protect yourself and fire, or get on a plane to elevate and get
higher.
We need to rise above the dirt that they throw at us and buy back our
communities.

Be You and You Will Be Free

Letting go of the grip of who you think I should be
Gripping to the person I am destined to be
I will say it once,
twice,
three times for the people who act as if they don't hear my voice
My melanin is popping
My love for women is as deep as my soul
And I am more woman than you have ever known
So what society sees is three strikes
But what I see is three rings of fire
Intense Powerful and as Real as real will ever come

Love conquers all. PLP

Embrace Your Pain

Pain we don't speak of it because we always let it fade away
But does it ever fade or do we just turn away?
Blink twice and it's back to stay, but again we say go away
We don't understand that we have to face our fears
We have to know that today it's pain, sorrow, and sadness
But today will be yesterday and we will smile again
So take it one second, one minute, one hour, one day at a time
Embrace and understand the sadness because when it comes again
you won't run away
You will stand tall and strong, mighty and proud
Because today is yesterday and the pain will fade away
Because you yourself have fought the pain head on
You closed your lips to the alcohol
You closed your legs to the pleasure that will create pain
You opened your mind, body, and spirit to the notion of everlasting
happiness
You received it all because you know one day you will be here again
But you will not hang your head down
You will lift and lift everyone around going through the same thing
Because you learned that love can hurt but it shouldn't hurt
Love heals. love conquers. love beats anything.

Black Lives Matter

HISstory has passed down with so many of lies
Each generation that receives these teachings constructs the idea of
beating b, lynching l, abusing a, choking c, and killing k.
If that went over your mind, the story undermines black, the very
souls that created the credit they took.
But matter cannot be created nor destroyed.
Or that is what is said because he cannot destroy what he could not
create
Because they tried to destroy the matter of black lives.
BLACK LIVES MATTER yesterday, today, and I promise you even
after days I can utter this phrase.

Spirituality Exists

You can't tell me that a higher power doesn't exist
And you can't tell me that my God would condemn me for loving
women and not you for your feelings
They gave you religion; my ancestors gave me spirituality
The shiver I get when my soul is spoken to
This is what I let change my views
If your heart is pure that means more than how much you step onto a
church floor
I am talking deeper than some of you may think
I am not down-playing your religion; I am trying to stop you from
pretending
Create connections from your core, so you can live a life that you
were called for.

Twenty-Two

Twenty-two has left me with so many memories
I learned to love myself to the core
Reach into my soul and make myself whole
My ancestors have been speaking to my soul like never before.
After everything I have experienced, now you calling me author P.
If I did not endure that pain, this gain wouldn't mean anything.
My success was composed in the fields where my ancestor's blood, sweat, and tears lay.

Paris Pruitt was born and raised in Hartford, Connecticut to parents dragged through the criminal justice system, which you may call criminals. She has nine siblings that have influenced her in different ways. She had the guidance of her very wise grandparents to teach morals, family values, and humility. She attends the University of Connecticut as a Biological Sciences major and is a first-generation college student.

Through self-discovery, she began to unleash her story through written word at the age of nine that was never exposed to anyone. Through the need to make a difference in communities of color, led her to become a member of Zeta Phi Beta Sorority, Incorporated. Through time, contemplation, and hard work she founded a non-profit organization, The I.M.P.R.I.N.T. Initiative, Inc, on August 11, 2017, to propel middle and high school scholars of color to discover their passions.

Her focus is to unshackle the pain that comes with holding in trauma for 22 years and let readers know that you are not alone. The purpose of "Unshackled" is to allow insight into the unleashing of pain. To show that it is okay and necessary to shed the hurt and trauma from your past.